DATE DUE

Jam Session

Terrell Davis

Terri Dougherty

ABDO Publishing Company

C 1   2003   14.95

visit us at
www.abdopub.com

Published by ABDO Publishing Company, 4940 Viking Drive, Suite 622, Edina, Minnesota 55435.
Copyright © 1999 by Abdo Consulting Group, Inc. International copyrights reserved in all countries. No part of this book may be reproduced in any form without written permission from the publisher.

Printed in the United States.

Cover and Interior Photo credits: AP/Wide World Photos

Edited by Denis Dougherty

Sources: Associated Press; Boys' Life; Knight-Ridder; Newsweek; Sport; Sports Illustrated; Sports Illustrated for Kids; The Sporting News

Library of Congress Cataloging-in-Publication Data

Dougherty, Terri.
   Terrell Davis / by Terri Dougherty.
      p. cm. -- (Jam Session)
  Includes index.
  Summary: Describes the personal life and football career of the star running back for the Denver Broncos.
   ISBN 1-57765-354-8 (hardcover)
   ISBN 1-57765-356-4 (paperback)
  1. Davis, Terrell, 1972- Juvenile literature. 2. Football players--United States Biography Juvenile literature. [1. Davis, Terrell, 1972-- . 2. Football players. 3. Afro-Americans Biography.] I. Title II. Series.
   GV939.D347D68 1999
   796.332'092--dc21
   [B]   99-23954
                                                CIP

Contents

Giving the Packers a Headache

Terrell Davis was ripping through the Green Bay Packers in Super Bowl XXXII. He popped into the end zone from the one-yard line to score Denver's first touchdown. Near the end of the first quarter it looked like he was ready to dance into the end zone again after taking a hand-off from quarterback John Elway.

Terrell burst forward but was stopped at the five-yard line by LeRoy Butler and Santana Dotson. When he got up after taking the pounding from the Packers defenders, everything was a blur. He went back to the huddle and tried to keep playing. He knew it wasn't the hit that had affected his eyes. It was the start of a very, very bad headache called a migraine.

"I blanked out, but I stayed in the game," Terrell said. "I noticed I couldn't see. I knew that was the onset of a migraine."

At first none of his teammates noticed anything wrong. Then tight end Shannon Sharpe noticed Terrell was having problems and sent him to the sideline. Team doctors gave Terrell medicine, and he went to the locker room to wait for the pain to go away. He had been bothered by migraines since he was seven, and he knew that the best thing to do was to be patient.

"It's like getting your head squeezed in a vise," Terrell said. "It's like a normal headache, only 10 times worse."

The pain eased, and Terrell came back into the game after halftime, ready to fight. "He came out and showed he was a warrior," Sharpe said.

Terrell bulldozed the Packers, gaining 157 yards on 30 carries despite missing the second quarter. He was the first player ever to rush for three touchdowns in a Super Bowl. He was honored as the game's Most Valuable Player as the Broncos upset the defending champions 31-24 on January 25, 1998, in Davis' hometown of San Diego.

"I ran every play as if it were the last one of the season," Terrell said. "I knew I had to be strong for this game because if we ran the ball on these guys we had a pretty good chance [to win]."

Terrell scoots by a Packer defender.

The way Terrell fought his way down the field made it look like he was born to play professional football. But his rise from unknown running back to superstar has been one of the biggest surprises in NFL history.

Growing Pains

Terrell grew up in a tough area of San Diego with his parents, Kateree and Joe, and his older brothers: Joe Jr., James, Bobby, and Terry, and an older half-brother, Reggie Webb.

Terrell adored his mother. "I never saw anyone with as much energy as my mother," Terrell said. "She was always doing something, working hard, and taking care of her family."

Terrell's father, however, had a stormy personality. He was in and out of jail throughout Terrell's childhood, serving time for robbery, grand theft, and a shooting incident. He drank and used drugs. When he wasn't serving time in prison, he was disciplining his sons with an iron fist.

When Terrell was about eight, his father came into the boys' bedroom at two a.m. after a night of drinking. He told Terrell and the three brothers he shared the room with to get out of bed and stand against the wall. He got out his gun and started shooting at the boys. The bullets hit the bedroom wall, above the boys' heads.

"I wasn't scared," Terrell said. "I knew he wasn't going to kill us. He wouldn't do that. He loved us too much."

Joe Davis had a good side. He always seemed to make it to his sons' football and baseball games. He could laugh and dance around the house with his family. Although Terrell hated the painful beatings his father gave him, he respected and loved him just the same. "My father was a wonderful man who loved us," Terrell said.

In addition to his rough father, Terrell also had to deal with horrible headaches that began to affect him when he was in second grade. First he would see a burst of light, then feel the awful pain.

Terrell, did you eat your Chunky Soup? Terrell and his mother joke around while shooting a commercial for Campbell's Soup.

"There wasn't any medication or anything we could give him," Kateree said. "I knew he was strong, but he was so brave, too."

Although Terrell had headaches he was still an all-around excellent athlete. He was a star running back on his Pop Warner football team.

Terrell's parents separated for a year and a half, and reunited in 1981. After that, Terrell's father softened a bit and stayed out of big trouble. But the good times only lasted until 1987. On April 17, Joe Davis died of a disease called lupus.

Terrell took the loss hard. "I just couldn't forget what happened to my dad," he said. He skipped classes at Morse High School. He didn't study or listen to his teachers. He had been a standout running back, but didn't even try out for the high school team. "I was just disobedient," Terrell said. "My teachers couldn't stand me. I can't blame them."

From Long Shot to Long Beach

Terrell's mom was disappointed with him. A voice inside Terrell told him he had to change his attitude if he was going to make anything of his life. One of his brothers had gone to jail and another became a father while in high school. Terrell didn't want to make the wrong choices.

"I watched my brothers do things that changed their lives for the worse, and I couldn't let that happen to me," Terrell said.

Terrell transferred from Morse High School to Lincoln High School before his junior year and started over. He went to summer school and didn't skip classes during the school year.

"Lincoln was where I always wanted to go anyway," Terrell said. "I liked the teachers. I got involved in extracurricular activities. I wrestled. I ran track."

The football team already had a featured running back, so Terrell volunteered to play noseguard on defense during his junior year. The next season he asked for a chance to run with the ball.

"Give me a shot. If I don't make it, I won't bother you anymore," Terrell told the coach. That season he rushed for 700 yards and his team made the city playoffs.

Terrell was hoping for a college scholarship, but big-time schools didn't notice him. His half-brother Reggie was a running back at Long Beach State, not far from San Diego.

"I was walking by the coaches' office one day, and I heard them talking," Reggie said. "They were saying they were having trouble finding running backs. I told them there was a pretty good running back at Lincoln High they should take a look at. I didn't mention that he was my brother."

The coaches at Long Beach liked what they heard about Terrell and offered him a scholarship. However, he still had a lot of work to do before he became a star.

Oh Brother, This Guy's Good

Terrell was "redshirted" his first year at Long Beach. He could practice with the team but couldn't play in games. He played running back the next season as a redshirt freshman, in the same backfield as his brother Reggie.

"He got me moved to fullback," Reggie said. "That was when I thought he might be really good. I was the tailback and taking it easy, not worrying about anything. I thought I had it made. Terrell beat me out."

Terrell Davis playing for the University of Georgia in 1994.

Terrell gained 262 yards that season and scored two touchdowns. But then Long Beach State dropped its football program. Terrell had to find a new place to play college ball.

The University of Georgia offered him a scholarship and he gladly accepted. He spent most of his first year at Georgia blocking for All-America running back Garrison Hearst, who also went on to play in the NFL.

Terrell ran for 824 yards his junior year. But a hamstring injury sidelined him for four games his senior year and he gained only 445 yards. Terrell still hoped to be chosen in the 1995 NFL draft.

It takes six Georgia Tech players to stop Terrell during a game in 1993.

He worked hard and tried to impress NFL scouts at workouts. He couldn't believe that someone wouldn't see his ability and willingness to take on challenges.

"At the end of my junior year, I was projected as the third back to be taken in the draft," Terrell said. "So how can you go from being someone who's projected third in the draft to what happened in my senior season? My stock dropped because I missed a few games, but that means I can't play anymore?"

Terrell explodes past South Carolina players.

Bucking Bronco

Terrell had to wait until the sixth round of the draft before he was finally chosen by Denver. There were 196 players selected ahead of him, including 20 running backs. "I don't think I had the kind of stats that pro scouts were looking for," Terrell said.

What the scouts couldn't see was his willingness to work to make the team. "We had no idea what we were getting," Denver coach Mike Shanahan said. "But his work ethic is incredible."

Even Terrell didn't know how far his drive would take him. "When Denver drafted me, I was just hoping to make the practice squad," Terrell said. "I could never have envisioned the success I've achieved."

Terrell thought he would be used as just another body for veterans to hit during training camp. Then everything changed in an exhibition game against San Francisco in Tokyo. While playing on special teams, Terrell made a tremendous, bone-crunching hit on kick returner Tyronne Drakeford.

"On that hit alone you just made the team," Broncos defensive tackle Michael Dean Perry told him.

"You don't think of a running back flattening somebody on the kickoff team," Sharpe said. "When he did that, we all looked at each other and said, 'We've got something special here.' After that, he kept moving up the depth chart every week until they couldn't keep him out of the lineup."

Terrell was the team's sixth-string running back when training camp started. But a week before the regular-season opener, he was named a starter. He proved he was worthy of the honor. He stunned opponents with his power, cutback moves, and ability to break tackles.

Terrell ran for 1,117 yards, becoming the lowest-drafted player in NFL history to rush for 1,000 yards his rookie season. He rushed for seven touchdowns and finished second to his friend Curtis Martin of New England for the NFL Offensive Rookie of the Year Award.

Instead of being bowled over by his success, he kept a level head. "To me I'm still Terrell," he said. "A lot of people see me different, but I don't see the world different."

**Terrell stretching out
before a game.**

No Sophomore Jinx

The next season Terrell was determined to prove his successful rookie year was no fluke. "For me, it's just gratifying that I'm able to excel at this level," Terrell said. "You know, I really didn't have any success in college or high school, so it amazes me that I'm at the highest level and I'm doing as well as I am. The fact that I've come from nowhere is my biggest motivation."

Running wasn't the only way Terrell impressed opponents. His blocking and receiving skills were getting noticed, too.

"I knew that because of my lack of speed, I had to compensate one way or another," he explained. "And catching the ball and blocking were two things I needed to do in order to play. I started to develop those skills in high school, and they helped me out a little bit in college and are now my greatest assets."

Terrell led the American Football Conference (AFC) in rushing with 1,538 yards that season and was selected for the Pro Bowl. He was also the team's third-leading receiver with 49 catches.

"Terrell has the soft hands that our offense requires," Shanahan said. "And when he's not catching the ball, he can be a devastating blocker in passing situations."

The Broncos won 12 of their first 13 games and finished the season 13-3. But they were upset 30-27 by the Jacksonville Jaguars in the divisional playoffs. -- Terrell felt awful and was more determined than ever to win a championship.

Terrell Davis barrels over a Kansas City Chiefs' defender.

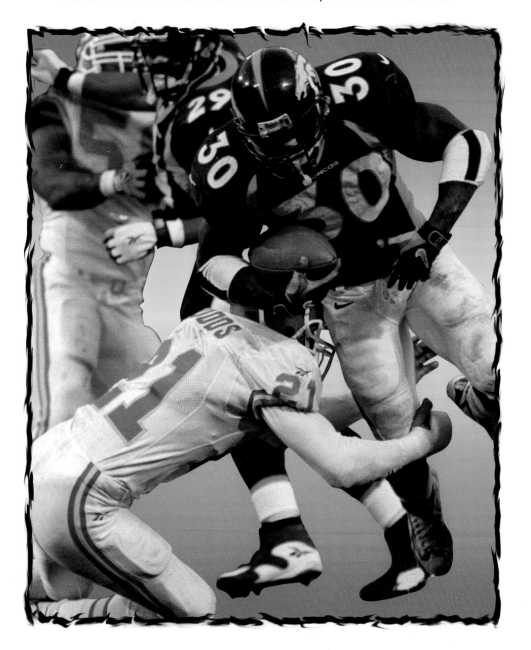

A Super Season

There was a lot of pressure on Terrell before the 1997 season. Some people thought he might gain 2,000 yards and be named the league's Most Valuable Player. There also was talk of Denver making it to the Super Bowl. The Broncos had lost in all four of their trips to football's most important contest.

"Without a doubt, I think I could be the difference between past Bronco Super Bowl teams and this team," Terrell said. "This is the type of team I look at and compare to past Super Bowl champions."

Denver's offense suited Terrell perfectly. Under the outstanding leadership of Elway, the Broncos made defenders cover wide areas and worry about both the run and pass.

"My rookie year, I was spooked playing against and with guys I had been in awe of, and it was totally uncomfortable," Terrell said. "My second year, I felt more like I belonged. Now I want to make things happen. I understand that this team is going to go places because of something I am doing."

Terrell became the fifth player in NFL history to rush for 1,000 yards in eight or fewer games. He pounded defenses like a sledgehammer. "He's very powerful and quick; he has good moves once he gets past the line (of scrimmage)," said Thurman Thomas, Buffalo's star running back. "He always falls forward."

Terrell gained 1,750 yards that season and continued to dominate in the playoffs. Against Pittsburgh in the AFC title game, he raced around the left end on his first carry for a 43-yard gain. Soon he was thundering into the end zone on an eight-yard run.

The Steelers hadn't allowed anyone to run for 100 yards all season. But Terrell gained 139 yards in the Broncos' 24-21 victory, which put them in the Super Bowl. Terrell scored eight touchdowns in the postseason—an NFL record. He ran for 581 yards in playoff wins over Jacksonville, Kansas City, Pittsburgh, and the Broncos' Super Bowl victory over the Green Bay Packers.

"The only thing that has shocked me so far is winning the Super Bowl," Terrell said the next season. "You can never envision yourself doing that."

The NFL's Brightest Star

Some players might have relaxed after winning the Super Bowl MVP Award. Not Terrell. He went to all the Broncos' off-season workouts. He arrived at 6 a.m. on weekends to run sprints and do bench presses and stomach crunches.

"People look at me differently now," Terrell said. "They view me as a guy who's been to a level that only the elite backs in the league have ever gotten to. If I go out there and have a bad season, I can't say, 'Well you have to remember I'm a sixth-round draft choice.' It used to be a surprise, the things I was doing. Now people expect it."

As a result of his hard work, Terrell got even better. In the second game of the season he gained 191 yards on 23 carries and scored three touchdowns in a 42-23 win over Dallas.

"He expects to make plays now that he didn't when he first came into the league," Shanahan said. "He knows he has a chance to dominate if he plays at the level he is on now."

Again there was talk that Terrell could gain 2,000 yards. He needed 170 yards against Seattle in the final game of the season. Although he was hurt, he fought off the pain and gained 178 yards on 29 carries. He was the fourth player in league history to top 2,000 yards in a season, but didn't take credit for the feat.

"With John back there throwing the ball, anybody could run for 2,000 yards," Terrell said.

Terrell was named the league's MVP. In addition to leading the league with 2,008 yards, he also led with 21 rushing touchdowns and 23 total touchdowns. He tied his former Georgia teammate Hearst for the league lead in yards per carry with a 5.1 average.

Terrell celebrates after scoring a touchdown.

In a divisional playoff game, Terrell gained 199 yards on 21 carries in a 38-3 victory over Miami. He had 167 yards and a 31-yard touchdown run in a 23-10 win over the New York Jets in the AFC Championship Game.

"Davis is one of the most exciting, explosive, dynamic, dominant running backs we have seen," said Bill Walsh, who won three Super Bowls as the 49ers coach. "His durability, his intensity, and his natural athletic ability are a blend of greatness."

Great things were expected of Terrell as Denver faced the Atlanta Falcons in Super Bowl XXXIII. He made some big runs that helped the Broncos take a 10-3 lead in the second quarter. But instead of using Terrell as a key player throughout the game, the Broncos used him mainly as a decoy. Because the Falcons focused their defense on stopping Terrell, the Broncos made big pass plays.

Terrell running over the Atlanta defense during Super Bowl XXXIII.

In the third quarter Elway and Terrell fooled the Atlanta defense. The defenders were set to stop Davis, but instead Elway threw an 80-yard touchdown pass to Rod Smith and the Broncos went ahead 17-3.

"I don't mind being a decoy at all," said Terrell, who still managed 102 yards on 25 carries. "I'll do what I need to do to help this team win championships."

Denver won 34-19 and Elway was named MVP. "We have a lot of key people on this team," said Terrell. "I'm just a piece of the puzzle."

Terrell races towards the end zone.

Back to the Future

Terrell has two Super Bowl rings, a Super Bowl MVP Award, and a regular-season MVP Award. But he's still a kid at heart. When he's not playing football, Terrell loves to play video games, bowl, and ride jet skis. "I'm the world's biggest little kid," he said. Terrell proved that when he appeared on the children's show *Sesame Street* and hung out with characters like Big Bird.

Terrell's mom lives right around the corner from his house in Aurora, Colorado. "I wouldn't want to go through what is happening to me without her sharing in it," Terrell said.

Terrell hasn't forgotten his former high school. He gave warm-up suits and shoes to Lincoln High's basketball team, and established a scholarship to send Lincoln students to college.

"I just want the kids to have a sense of hope," Terrell said. "I remember when I went to Lincoln, a lot of kids in my circle were just living day to day. I want to be a role model for these kids. I'm trying to lead a path for others to follow."

On the football field Terrell's as determined as ever. Medicine has helped him keep his headaches away, but his thundering runs are a big headache for opponents. He never wastes time looking for an opening. He makes his cut and surges forward with his legs churning.

His coach and teammates expect Terrell to be a powerful force for many years. "A lot of great players, once they've made it, haven't adhered to what got them there," Shanahan said. "That isn't going to happen to Terrell. He's never forgotten where he came from, and he'll never forget where he's going."

"Davis has always been tough," Elway said. "But we've just seen the early stages of how good he's going to be."

Terrell and Big Bird salute each other.

Terrell's Stats

Terrell Davis Profile

Height: 5-foot-11

Weight: 210 pounds

Birthdate: Oct. 28, 1972

Hometown: San Diego, California

Home: Aurora, Colorado

Family: Mother (Kateree) and five brothers: Joe Jr., James, Reggie, Bobby, and Terry

Personal: Terrell's favorite sport to participate in, other than football, is bowling. He likes watching basketball, playing video games, sleeping, and eating soul food and cheesecake. His favorite color is blue.

Honors and Achievements

- *Football Digest* NFL Rookie of the Year (1995)

- Pro Bowl alternate (1995)

- Associated Press NFL Offensive Player of the Year (1996, 1998)

- *Sports Illustrated* NFL Player of the Year (1996)

- All-Pro selection (1996, 1997, 1998)

- AFC rushing leader (1996, 1997, 1998)

- Pro Bowl selection (1996, 1997, 1998)

- AFC Player of the Year (1997)

- Super Bowl XXXII Most Valuable Player (January 1998)

- NFL rushing leader (1998)

- NFL Most Valuable Player (1998)

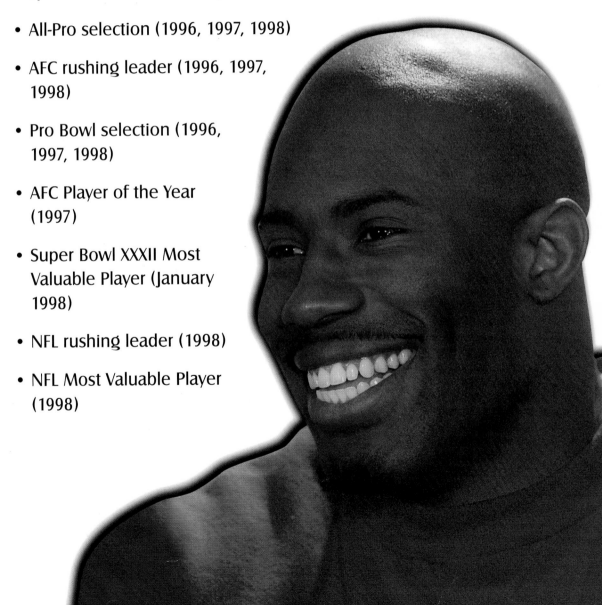

Records

- Became lowest-drafted player to rush for 1,000 yards in his rookie season (1995)

- Most rushing yards (2,476) in a season—including postseason—(1998), breaking his own record (2,331) set in 1997.

- Most rushing attempts (495) in a season—including postseason—(1997)

- Most touchdowns in one postseason, eight (1997)

- Most rushing touchdowns in one postseason, eight (1997)

- Most rushing touchdowns in a Super Bowl, three (January, 1998)

- Most consecutive 100-yard rushing games in the postseason, seven (1997-98)

Terrell holds the Lombardi Trophy after beating Green Bay 31-24 in Super Bowl XXXII on January 25, 1998.

Terrell Davis'
Season Rushing Totals

Year	Carries	Yards	Avg.	TDs
1995	237	1,117	4.7	7
1996	345	1,538	4.5	13
1997	369	1,750	4.7	15
1998	392	2,008	5.1	21

Terrell Davis'
Postseason Rushing Totals

Year	Carries	Yards	Avg.	TDs
1996	14	91	6.5	1
1997	112	581	5.2	8
1998	78	468	6.0	3

The NFL's 2,000-Yard Rushers

Player	Team	Year	Yards	Avg.
Eric Dickerson	L.A. Rams	1984	2,105	5.6
Barry Sanders	Detroit	1997	2,053	6.1
Terrell Davis	**Denver**	**1998**	**2,008**	**5.1**
O.J. Simpson	Buffalo	1973	2,003	6.0

Terrell Davis Chronology

1972 - Born in San Diego, California on Oct. 28.

1990 - Graduates from Lincoln High School in San Diego. Plays football on a scholarship at Long Beach State.

1992 - Transfers to University of Georgia.

1995 - Selected by Denver Broncos in sixth round of NFL draft and becomes lowest-drafted rookie ever to rush for 1,000 yards.

1996 - Leads AFC in rushing and is named the Associated Press NFL Offensive Player of the Year.

1997 - Leads AFC in rushing and is named Most Valuable Player in Super Bowl XXXII after leading Denver to a victory over Green Bay.

1998 - Leads NFL in rushing with 2,008 yards, is named the NFL's MVP and helps Broncos win their second consecutive Super Bowl.

Glossary

BACKFIELD - Group of players whose positions are behind the line of scrimmage. Offensive backfield includes quarterback, fullback, and running back. Defensive backfield includes cornerbacks and safeties.

DRAFT - The National Football League's method of allowing teams to choose players from college teams.

EXTRACURRICULAR - Student activities connected with school but conducted outside the regular school day.

MVP - Most Valuable Player. The MVP Award is given to the top player in the NFL each season.

PRO BOWL - The NFL's postseason all-star game.

QUARTERBACK - The player on offense who calls the signals for the plays and gets the snap from the center. He can run, pass, hand the ball to a teammate, or pitch the ball to a teammate.

REDSHIRT - College athlete who can practice with the team but can't compete in games for a season.

RUNNING BACK - Offensive player who lines up behind the quarterback and usually runs with the ball. Can also block and catch passes.

SCHOLARSHIP - A gift given to designated students to allow them to attend a college for reduced or no cost.

SPECIAL TEAMS - Units of players that play during extra point, kickoff, punt and field-goal situations.

TOUCHDOWN - Scoring six points by carrying the ball over an opponent's goal line, or catching or recovering the ball in an opponent's end zone.

Index